BRIGHT STAR

INSPIRATIONAL POETRY FOR CHRISTMAS & OTHER
BEGINNINGS

TWELVE POEMS TO INSPIRE GIFT BOOKS
BOOK ONE

ORNA ROSS

FontPublications

FONT PUBLICATIONS IS THE PUBLISHING IMPRINT FOR ORNA ROSS'S FICTION AND POETRY, THE
GO CREATIVE! BOOKS AND PLANNERS AND ALLIANCE OF INDEPENDENT AUTHORS PUBLISHING
GUIDES.
ALL ENQUIRIES: SARAH@ORNAROSS.COM

* * *

BRIGHT STAR
Inspirational Poetry for Christmas & Other Beginnings
E-book: 978-0-957341-22-7
Paperback: 978-1-913588-86-1
Large Print: 978-1-913349-79-0
Hardback: 978-1-913349-80-6
Audiobook: 978-1-913349-99-8

❋ Created with Vellum

PRAISE FOR BRIGHT STAR

"A lovely, emotional collection, something to treasure."

— THE BOOK WORMERY

"A gorgeous collection of poetry...for everyone. It speaks to what this season is like and when I turned the final page I felt solace and calm and hopeful. This book would make a wonderful Christmas gift for a loved one, or a lovely treat for yourself. I highly recommend this one!"

— RATHERTOOFONDOFBOOKS.COM

"These writings reflect that...never-ending quest for a chink of eternal light in the darkness. This is an understandably slim volume... but to me, not an inveterate poetry reader, that makes it more accessible, more appealing, than a weightier tome... If you manage to steal the time to read one poem a day over the 12 days of festivities, this book provides a stimulating, contemplative reward."

— AMAZON.COM CUSTOMER

"Beautifully presented, thoughtful, slim (easy to post!) anthology that makes a super Christmas present."

— AUTHOR DEBBIE YOUNG.

For all the Christmas lovers.

"The beginning is always today."

— *MARY SHELLEY*

CONTENTS

INTRODUCTION

BRIGHT STAR

*B*right Star is the first book in the *Twelve Poems to Inspire* series, poetry gift books for special events and occasions. While offering one poem a day for each of the twelve days of Christmas, the book is spiritual rather than Christian, exploring the theme of blessings and beginnings from a dozen different angles.

Where I live now in the south-east corner of England, and where I grew up in the south-east corner of Ireland, the late December holiday falls in mid-winter. The nights are at their longest, with lamplight, candles and firelight providing perfect conditions for reading. Perhaps where you live, you have Christmas on the beach? No matter. This book is designed for gifting during the gifting season, yes, but also at any time of birth, rebirth or beginning anew.

For 2000 years, millions of people have told the story of what happened in the town of Bethlehem, but stories of longing for quiet and light pre-date and post-date it. Today, as we absorb stories as pixels and moving images, still we seek what the ancients sought.

We complain about the commercialisation of the season, and wonder why in our multicultural, secular countries, we still observe the religious rituals, but each year, most of us succumb, obediently flocking to family hearths. A feast is served. Lights are lit. Carols are sung. Prayers are said. Our relatives, especially our children, are honored with gifts. Why?

Jesus of Nazareth was born, the story says, in a lowly stable, under a bright star, on a still night. Son of a single-mother, meek and mild, protected by the kindness of strangers and beasts, and the adoration of the wise for that other-worldly, invisible power: the creative spirit that births all, without seed of man. This spirit, the story tells us, is found in learned kings and loving carpenters, in tame animals and angelic babies, in you, and me, in all that is. In this reading, nativity becomes a great symbol of possibility. Anything can happen at the moment of birth.

We know this intellectually, but to live and act from this knowledge is something else. In the heart of darkness, how do we find a bright star of light to follow? That is the question the festive season asks each year.

Through preparing our food and favors, through giving our gifts, through communion with our family and friends, we demonstrate our answer. Whether we're marking the Christian Christmas, pre-Christian *yule*, Chinese *Dongzhi*, Jewish *Hanukkah*, Hindi *Makaraa Sankrānti*, we mark the December solstice as a celebration of birth and rebirth.

We can take refuge in the meaning of this season at any moment of beginning anew—which, of course, is every moment. We can always start over. Anything can happen, anytime. I wish you all the potential of possibility, every day of the year.

Sonas leat!
Orna

BRIGHT STAR

POEMS TO INSPIRE GIFT BOOKS: BOOK I

REBIRTH

Night and Day
Soaring
First Flush

NIGHT AND DAY

"The great clock of the sky is revolving..."

NIGHT AND DAY

Call it a day. The great clock of the sky
is freewheeling towards dusk,
secreting its shadows
around every living thing.
The shout of life
that was this day
is being quieted to dream.

Cast away. The great clock
of the sky is revolving
in reverie,
bestowing dark wisdom
upon every sleeping thing.
The balm of night
is soothing days'
doings to dream.

Counter sway. The great clock
of the sky is spiralling
into dawn,
unveiling light rising
within every waking thing.
The shout of life
that is tomorrow
being born out of dream.

* * *

SOARING

…"in repeat, all down the street, the Christmas angels soar…"

SOARING

In dank-dark afternoons
air that tastes of sleet,
we dodge between the growls
of taxis, buses, cars, as from work
to shops we go, intent on lists
food, and clothes, and gifts, and then…
just as it all begins to feel too grim,
the Christmas lights go on.
Strings and wings of angel shine
shimmering their promise:
unimaginable as warmth may be
today, sun will return to radiate.
Scents of summer will, all willing,
be sniffed through skin again,

We barely own them, these memory
slivers of a future life of light.
All we can see for now is how,
outside the station, high above
the city people noise,
suspended by long lines of light
(just as they were last year,
and the year before)
forever in the act of taking off,
and in repeat, all down the street,
the Christmas angels soar.

* * *

FIRST FLUSH

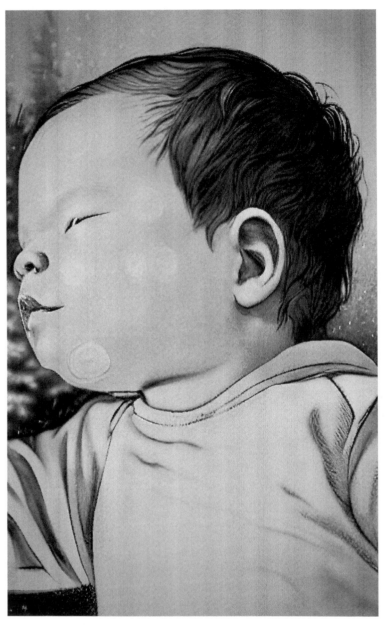

"…your gossamer brows, your tight-shut eyes, …"

FIRST FLUSH

Not yet one day old.

As we, with your mother, stare,
aching at the soft throb
of your vulnerable skull,
your neck too slight, as yet,
to hold your head but already
elegant, like hers;

as we gaze with a wonder
last felt thirty years before
at your tiny nails,
each one of ten a pin-point
of pure perfection
on your cupped feet and fingers,

the sun comes out,
emerging from clouds unnoticed
until sunlight passes,
for the first time,

across your shut-tight eyes,
your light-blue lids,
your dark-drawn brows,
and we are each illuminated,
all newborn.

* * *

RECONNECT

THE SHORTEST DAY

"...through the solstice silence calls..."

THE SHORTEST DAY

Amid toils and tills the shortest day
slips into light, grey-misted.
Dawn to noon soft rising,
hardly here, away it slides.

Shops lay on feast food and drink,
presents, music, trinkets.
Outside damp crowds, in silhouette,
beneath slate-tinted skies.

Small birds, breathy, sing it out
from the tips of thinning branches,
as through the solstice silence calls
louder than any noise.

* * *

BRIGHT STAR

"Pierce through our darkness, o bright star…"

BRIGHT STAR

O lady from clear realms afar,
dream-bright the power of your good will.
Your nascent light in us instil.
Pierce through our darkness, o bright star.

These days, to spread ways we hold good,
we send out troops to foreign lands,
our youth in troops of comrade bands,
to sunder flesh and splatter blood.

Dear bearer of the soft borne realm,
once more with kindness turn the till.
With your mild eyes see through our shill.
Help us to render up this helm.

Within us secret hatreds rage,
our children's breath falls foul or ill
raised on the death of what we kill,
and all that we destroy and cage.

O lady from clear dreams afar
Call forth the power of our good will.
Our grail of light in us fulfil.
Dispel our darkness, o bright star.

* * *

LONG LIGHT

"Long light lives by grace of shadow…"

LONG LIGHT

Every light creates a shadow, the stars
can't shine without the night.
Seek to muffle up your sorrow:
feel life fade inside and out.

Loose it. Let it sear you hollow,
prise you open, clear your throat.
Long light lives by grace of shadow.
The stars are pleased to shine through night.

* * *

RENEW

Beholden
Awakening
These Times

BEHOLDEN

"Oh stars… your hearts exploding into dust, somehow making us."

BEHOLDEN

On my back in the dark.
given up to night, I lie,
a fool aground. A suckling.
yearning, turning in want
and will, smothering in the urges
of the underneath.

Up there, the spangled stars,
the moon, one-quarter lit and on
the wane, hiding its hollows,
and the black beyond. That dark
that shades the darkness.

Night pulls me in.
Night holds me still.
Night holds my wants
against my will,
until I am upended,
released to rise again.

Held, I hold. The stars, shining in
from forever ago, unfathomable
in their million millions
(why so many?) and in their age
(*how* old?) Their hearts exploding
into dust somehow making us?

The moon, so cratered
and so constant in its change.
Growing darkness in each month's
declining shine, showing how

all fullness fades to shade.
(Though just for three days.)

The darkness, that sets all the light
alight, our dear good night.
Its milky ways of silken stars;
its mingled shades of ink between
and all I've said and felt and done.
All held. All level held. All level
and forever held, here,
in my own holding
in the empyrean.

AWAKENING

"This moment can be Christmas./A fantastical conceit…"

AWAKENING

This moment can be Christmas.
A fantastical conceit: a holy birth
without the thrusting seed of man.
A humble beginning, protected
by the kindness of a stranger,
warmed by kindly beasts,
understood and adored by the wise.

Or it can pass, unwoken.

While you push your advances
you are also, always,
the child of surrender.

This moment can be a star
in the making: daily dust and gas
collapsing into the gravity of being,
so it can rise and shine across
twenty-five trillion miles.

Or it can pass, unwoken.

While you resist the pull of earth
you are also, always,
a mother to the stars.

This moment can be savoured
in your own body, known to be more
fully you for not being all your own.

Or it can pass, unwoken.

While you battle against yourself,
you are also, always,
a sister to the clouds.

This moment can be a parent
tending to the cries of the kids
setting their daily world to rights, knowing
they will have their hearts crucified,
no matter what you do but doing it.
Knowing they will be taken down
but will rise again, as long as they bow
to the great beckoning beyond.
Offering them presence and belief.

Or it can pass, unwoken.

While you journey hard,
you are also, always,
the daughter of arrival.

This moment can be Christmas.
A fantastical conceit: a holy birth
without the thrusting seed of man.
A humble birth, protected
by the kindness of a stranger,
warmed by kindly beasts,
understood and adored by the wise.
Or it can pass, unwoken.

* * *

THESE TIMES

"Earth ...sends up her wake-up calls..."

THESE TIMES

"This too will pass,"
the ancients said
and so it did
but so too did it stay
within the human race
in memories
if not in ways.

And so we've come
to here,
this surface blur
called now,
its depths though
a clear echo.
Listen. Hear.

Earth still holds out her arms
as she sends up
her wake-up calls.
She knows.

And we born of the earth,
her seas and stars, know too.
Can we bear to plunge
into the wound and find
the pearl: the question
passed to us?

What can we make
and mend
to make amends?

We have, now, what we need
and the whole world
has shown how
it can act as one.
The time is come.

REJOICE

The Calling
Mid-Winter Benediction
Christmas Rain

THE CALLING

THE CALLING

I have come to you now.
Open your ears
the pores of your skin
the blades of your back.
Unself yourself.

I have come
because I know you
and it is time.

Let go of your pathways.
I have brought you thus far.
I do not want to abandon you
on the road.

Listen. My sound is like
the praise prayer of a lover.
It can raise you above the moon.
Its pulse is calling you up
through the underbelly swell of the tide
the hidden side of the clouds
the wing face of the wind.

Yes, I am asking you to fly.
Have I not given you the skies?

* * *

MID-WINTER BENEDICTION

"Bless trees that broke the gnaw of wind..."

MID-WINTER BENEDICTION

Father, mother, growing child,
all blessings on you all.
Bless your hearth, and bless your board,
and every sturdy wall.

Bless the fields about your place,
the hillock and the sedge.
Bless holly bush and laurel
and birdsong from the hedge.

Bless the air on hands and face,
and sun on winter's day.
Bless trees that broke the gnaw of wind,
and heralded the way.

Bless your open windows
letting moon and starlight in.
Bless unlatched door that welcomed
a stranger as if kin.

Bless the roof that shelters you,
the cribs on which you rest,
bless the holding of your house,
yes, all your lintels blessed.

Bless bow and fiddle tuning,
for carols soon to sing.
Bless drink to fire some dancing,
and fire to warm the skin.

Bless news fetched in by neighbours,

all tidings that they bring,
bless feast laid out for feasting,
let merriment begin.

Bless the joy here gathering,
Its life within us ring,
Oh, bless the heart and soul
of every living, blessed thing.

Blessed the hearth, and blessed the board,
and blessed each sturdy wall.
Mother, father, growing child,
all blessings on you all.

CHRISTMAS RAIN

"...this ceaseless rainfall on the town..."

CHRISTMAS RAIN

In the year's dying days,
rainfall is falling, failing to freeze.
No white Christmas again
this year, just the relentless rain,
hard and silent, you said,
as a Christmas suicide.

I know it hurts your soul,
this ceaseless rainfall on the town
and across the fields of forest trees
raised for the season.
Fir and spruce grown to be cut.
No sooner born than dying,
then dumped, you said, reminding
us again of those who'll spend
the season ill or afraid,
failing or alone.

It's true, it's true,
the trees are killed,
in the name of human life:
faith and hope and charity,
friends and fun and family,
hymns and prayers and superfluity
of food and drink and gifts,
abundance of all the worldly goods.

I am not blind to what that does,
but, oh my dear, is it not also true
that in the spangled homes,
the valiant trees are letting loose

their pine scent, as the darkening
world spins round again
towards the sun's returning?

Whatever we think or know,
most of us will loop our pearls
of light and tinsel round a bough,
hang baubles of colour from
its needled branches, and top off
the confection with a sharply-pointed star,
then step out into the winter air
to join the jingle. And look!

Come outside! It looks like the rain
is slowing, and soon might touch
our cheeks soft feather light,
as it freezes white.

LET'S KEEP IN TOUCH

Enjoyed the poems? Would you like more? If you're online, we have lots of ways to continue the poetic conversation.

UPDATES & BONUSES

My monthly email brings you my inspirational poetry news and ideas, discounted books, and other pen-friend presents. Follow the link below to become my poetry pen-friend get **free e-books.**

OrnaRoss.com/Free-Poetry

PLEASE REVIEW THIS BOOK ONLINE

If you enjoyed this book, please give it a quick review online by visiting the link below and selecting the "Reviews" tab. Your review doesn't have to be long or detailed. A quick star rating and a sentence or two that helps others to understand the value of this book is all that's needed. I appreciate the support more than you know. *Go raibh maith agat!*

OrnaRoss.com/BrightStar

BECOME A PATRON

For a small investment, you can become a direct patron of the arts! You make a small monthly payment to support my work and I send you a welcome gift, and a poetry e-book each month and my poetry news. You can also opt in for more, at higher levels of support. More info: Orna-Ross.com/Poetry-Patrons

AWARD-WINNING
INSPIRATIONAL POETRY

Treat yourself to more poetry

Browse and buy more inspirational poetry books on my website:
OrnaRoss.com/Poetry-Books

ACKNOWLEDGMENTS

My thanks to Jane Dixon-Smith for cover design of this book and the *Twelve Poems to Inspire* series.

To the #IndiePoetryPlease community on Instagram, thank you for reading, thank you for writing.

To the publishing team: Sarah Begley, Kayleigh Brindley and Dan Parsons, who get the words from me to the readers.

Thanks to the creators of the AI art tool Dream, app. wombo.art, which generates artwork from lines of the poems. A dream indeed. AI generated art, like AI generated text, is only possible by standing on the shoulders of all the other writers and artists. Womba gives a special thank you to Geoffrey Hintonk Jürgen Schmidhuber, RiversHaveWings Boris Day, OpenAI and Stability AI... and so do I.

To Philip Lynch, for being my first reader and sometime muse.

And a special thanks to my poetry patrons, who keep the poems coming.

With a bow, thank you all. *Sonas libh go léir*.

x Orna

ABOUT THE POET

Orna Ross is an award-winning self-published novelist and poet, and founder of the Alliance of Independent Authors (ALLi). Enjoying book sales in 120+ countries worldwide, she has won several awards and her work for ALLi has seen her named "one of the 100 most influential people in publishing" (The Book-seller). Born in Waterford and raised in Wexford, in the south-east corner of Ireland, she now lives and works in London and St Leonard's-on-Sea, in the south-east corner of England.

Find out more at
OrnaRoss.com

amazon.com/Orna-Ross/e/B001K86OBA
goodreads.com/OrnaRoss
patreon.com/OrnaRoss